MARY, FIRST DISCIPLE

MARY, FIRST DISCIPLE

REFLECTIONS ON MARY OF NAZARETH

Bishop Thomas J. Grady

Pauline
BOOKS & MEDIA
BOSTON

ISBN 0-8198-4806-9

Design: Tracey Matthia Dugas, FSP

Illustrations by Carol Granstrom Stanton

Printed and published in the U.S.A. by Pauline Books & Media, 50 Saint Pauls Avenue, Boston, MA 02130-3491.

www.pauline.org

Pauline Books & Media is the publishing house of the Daughters of St. Paul, an international congregation of women religious serving the Church with the communications media.

1 2 3 4 5 6   04 03 02 01 00 99

To Mary
Who Believed
in the
Word

Contents

FOREWORD

"Hail Mary, full of grace! The Lord is with you." In this familiar phrase the words of Sacred Scripture meet with centuries of Catholic piety. Together they yield a truth which requires us to use our hearts and minds to understand. A wholly intellectual approach to the person of Mary fails to grasp the mystery of divine grace enveloping her existence from her conception to her assumption. A wholly affective approach leaves unsatisfied the human consciousness—also God's precious gift—and the need to speak our faith in ways intelligible to every generation.

These two approaches, intellectual and affective, are represented in the prayer, "Hail Mary, full of grace! The Lord is with you." The mystery of grace which filled Mary exists only partially within our human experience and so is only partially available to rational inquiry. Just as mystics have always found that words escape them as they approach the depths of divine life, and philosophers have discovered that "the heart has its reasons which reason cannot know" (Blaise Pascal), so too the mystery of Mary's grace-filled life escapes us unless we see with our hearts and our minds.

The words, "The Lord is with you," remind us that all of Mary's life and her meaning for us derives from her relationship to Jesus. In the tradition of the Catholic Church, Mary is the person most closely united to the mystery of saving grace that is her Son, Jesus. She most perfectly accepted God's gift of grace and for this reason she occupies a unique place as the highest of all God's creation.

Mary has been redeemed just as we have. She is not on a par with Jesus, but depends on him for all that she is. She is not the Creator, but the highest of creatures. She does not rival the Spirit for a place in the Trinity, but remains the humble and courageous woman overshadowed by the Spirit.

The Catholic Church has always distinguished between the saving work of the Lord and Mary's unique role in salvation history. But because popular piety has sometimes blurred the two, occasionally the Church has had to restate the Catholic faith in this regard. In clarifying the authentic teaching the Church wishes especially to present a genuine devotion to Mary for each generation and culture. Thus the Second Vatican Council says:

> *Redeemed, in a more exalted fashion, by reason of the merits of her Son, and united to him by a close and indissoluble tie, she is endowed with the high office and dignity of the Mother of the Son of God, and therefore she is also the beloved daughter of the Father and the temple of the Holy Spirit.*
>
> *Because of this gift of sublime grace, she far surpasses all creatures, both in heaven and on earth. But being of the race of Adam, she is at the same time also united to all those who are to be saved. Indeed, she is clearly the mother of the members of Christ...since she has by her love joined in bringing about the birth of believers in the Church, who are members of its head.*
>
> *Wherefore she is hailed as pre-eminent and as a wholly-unique member of the Church, and as its type and outstanding model in faith and charity. The Catholic Church, taught by the Holy Spirit, honors her with filial affection and devotion as a most beloved mother* (Dogmatic Constitution on the Church, *n. 53).*

The Vatican Council chose chapter eight of *The Dogmatic Constitution on the Church* as the most appropriate place to treat devotion to Mary. In this way Mary is presented as closely tied to both Christ and the Spirit who continues the work of salvation in every time and place. Clearly the Council members intended to establish Mary as a sign of God's saving grace in the universe, a sign that has helped centuries of believers as they find in her answers to questions regarding their relationship to God.

May the following reflections on Mary, the Mother of God, help the minds and hearts of readers to follow her according to the richness of our Catholic faith.

> *Let the faithful remember that true devotion consists neither in sterile or transitory affection, nor in a certain vain credulity, but proceeds from true faith, by which we are led to recognize the excellence of the Mother of God, and we are moved to a filial love for our mother and to imitate her virtues* (Dogmatic Constitution on the Church, *n. 67*).

Father Rob Garafalo

The First Disciple

She was the first—

First to know
what God was about in the world.

First to share with God's Son
the brokenness of humanity

Making for him a home,
a warm place,
a place of love

Watching him pass,
bent and bloody,
Seeing the last drop
of blood and water

Alone
Battlement of Silver,
love stronger than death.

Heartful giving her flesh
heart—torn giving herself to the Word.

First to believe the world's salvation

The first disciple.

FIRST REFLECTION

A DISCIPLE TRULY FREE

On that first Christmas night there was no Gospel, no New Testament, no supportive Christian community of believers, no Church or Tradition, no great Christian minds like Augustine or Aquinas to interpret the marvelous events.

Alone, Mary faced the great mystery that had come into her life. This young woman—hardly more than a girl—was about to give birth to a child. She rode a donkey beside Joseph as they traveled from Nazareth, down toward Jerusalem, and beyond to Bethlehem. While Joseph helped Mary on the long road, he couldn't help her with the mystery, the child and the new direction to her life. He could only believe, trust and stand ready with his love.

God had asked Mary to be mother of the "child

savior" whose kingdom would never end, a virgin mother under the overshadowing of the Spirit of God.

How could she believe the message really came from God? What would it mean to bear a child conceived of God's Spirit? What would Joseph think? What would the people think? Could a child of *hers* be savior? Could the king of all ages be conceived on a quiet, lonely hillside of Nazareth? *Where would this mystery lead her?*

Mary said yes. Unhindered by the fear of risk or self-interest, Mary's freedom was in her ability to listen—to be attentive and completely open to God. Her freedom was in her capacity to accept the Word of God into her life.

Even in the company of other travelers and with Joseph beside her, Mary walked a lonely road to Bethlehem. All those Christmas cards with her picture, the Gothic cathedrals in her honor, the Renaissance paintings and marble statues of her did not yet exist. She only saw a dreary road stretching ahead and felt the weariness of the journey and the jolting of the donkey beneath her. Joseph's guiding hand rested gently on hers but it could not dispel her anxious question: "Where will my child be born?" God's creative power led Mary one small step at a time through the uncertainties in her life and to a deeper understanding of the mystery within her womb.

The journey took several days and they must have stopped somewhere for the night. Mary and Joseph probably lodged in a typical caravansary of the time: a sort of open air courtyard with a narrow roof along the walls. The travelers cooked in the open and they slept against the walls, under the stars.

Indistinguishable among the forms huddled against the walls slept the woman whom God found lovely, the woman whom he favored above all women. Mary, the fairest daughter of a chosen people, beautiful as a bride—as God's bride. Mary, beautiful as a young mother-to-be—God's mother-to-be.

Perhaps during the night she felt the child move within her, his heart beating next to hers. The stars watching over the travelers knew her secret. From her—a poor, hidden, worried woman—the sun would rise and the light would shine upon the world.

Along the road to Bethlehem, Mary, Our Lady of Advent, comes to each of us with an incomparable understanding of the human condition. She bears the gift of her Son, God's beauty made visible through her flesh. A true devotion to Mary does not remove her from our ordinary human experiences; it does not elevate her above life's sufferings and concerns. Because Mary struggled just as we do, she can relate to our human experiences.

The New Testament portrays Mary as a model disciple. She received a wonderful promise from the Lord, believed in it and lived up to it. Christian living challenges us to do the same: to accept God's word in our hearts, and live as though we really believe his promises to us.

> My soul gives praise to the Lord,
> and my spirit rejoices in God my Savior;
> Because he had regard for the lowliness of
> his handmaid,
> behold, henceforth all generations shall call
> me blessed,
> For the Mighty One has done great things
> for me,
> and holy is his name,
> And his mercy is from generation to genera-
> tion
> toward those who fear him.
>
> (Lk 1:46–50)

PRAYER

Gentle and loving God, we proclaim your greatness, for you have looked upon us with all our frailty and limitations and have blessed us beyond our hopes and dreams. You who are mighty have worked wonders in our lives. You who are all powerful have not shown us judgment but mercy.

And so we bless you, Lord God of all creation, and our spirits rejoice in your loving presence. For you are our God, and you have truly blessed us.

ADVENT

Southward the journey was long,
many miles, many days.

She was burdened.
In her womb a child,
Master of the universe.

Their goal a stable in Bethlehem
straw in a manger.

Until then she was straw
golden straw
for the Master of the universe.

Eternal Light
hidden in the darkness of her womb
waiting for dawn.

Joseph, ordinary man on an ordinary road
pilgrim to a stable.

Walking with God and God's chosen one

Tell me, Joseph, other ordinary one,
how to say Mary, to say Jesus,
to journey with them.

How to be ready for Dawn.

SECOND REFLECTION

A DISCIPLE OF OBEDIENCE

When we think of Mary just before she was invited to become the Mother of God, we can say that God found her beautiful. We can even say that God made her beautiful. But Mary's beauty, a gift from God, was not so much her personal, external attributes, as it was her attitude of readiness. Mary stood ready and willing to accomplish her part in God's plan for the redemption and salvation of humanity.

In the Gospel of Saint Luke the archangel Gabriel greets Mary with the words: "Hail, full of grace." The Greek word for grace, *charis,* implies a sense of joy. God rejoices over and delights in one whom he has graced. Because God has graced Mary with the fullness of *charis,* he greatly delights in Mary.

Various translations of the Gospel account of Gabriel's words at the annunciation read: "full of grace," "O highly favored daughter," and "so highly favored." The last two indicate most clearly that Mary's *charis* is not something she *has,* but a gift God has *given* her.

The second part of Gabriel's greeting: "The Lord is with you," indicates that it is God who favors her. It is not the ordinary greeting of, "The Lord be with you," but it positively declares that the Lord *is* with her. God favored Mary so that more than any other person in human history, she would play a special role to fulfill the messianic promises.

Mary was asked to make the most important decision in human history: "Will you become the mother of the messiah, the Son of God?" She replied: "Behold the handmaid of the Lord; let it be done to me according to your word" (Lk 1:38). In faith, Mary accepted God's plan. But she was a human being, albeit a human person highly favored by God; nevertheless, she acted in a human way. She asked how this could be and then gave her response.

Is it possible to imitate a woman as perfect as Mary? Yes, it is possible because Mary simply did what we are all called to do. God gave Mary a role in bringing Christ's truth and salvation into the world. She cooperated with Christ in God's plan for the salvation of all people.

In the same way, God invites each one of us to use the unique gifts he has given us to build up his kingdom here on earth. Certainly God highly favored Mary, who participated in his plan more uniquely than any other human person. Yet God has favored us all in many ways. Like Mary we can participate in his plan of salvation. Graced by God, we can place our gifts at the service of the Church and one another. Mary gave us an excellent example for doing so.

But was Mary too submissive? Can she be a model for people today, who value independence and self-fulfillment? Mary's attitude of surrender to God does not mean passivity or a lack of a sense of personal autonomy and worth. Today's society values self-fulfillment and autonomy, but it recognizes limits to individuality, autonomy and self-fulfillment. We must take into account the rights and even the hopes of others and recall the deep-seated human need for love and intimacy. As an autonomous, free individual Mary made a difficult decision of extraordinary importance with serene trust in God.

Mary
consented to
God's coming alive in the world
through her.

Mary believed God was asking her to be the mother of his only-begotten Son. In saying yes to God, Mary risked the social reactions to her being a mother before living with Joseph. She risked Joseph's response and possible rejection because of her pregnancy. Above all, she courageously risked being a part of God's mysterious plan as mother of the messiah and all that would mean. She made her decision freely and stood by it for a lifetime despite the uncertainties and the difficulties.

Mary freely surrendered to God. As creatures made in the image of God and sustained by him, we too must surrender to God's loving providence. By the nature of our being, we relate to God as creature to Creator. God has absolute authority over us; our being requires obedience to God, for it expresses our creaturehood. God, who is infinite love and mercy, shows his authority as a loving father and mother might. God so loved all humanity that his only Son became one of us in order to reveal the Father and to redeem us. And Christ, the revelation of God, said: "I have come down from heaven not to do *my* will, but to do the will of him who sent me" (Jn 6:38).

Openness to God's will, to his love and mercy in our lives, brings us true happiness. Mary models that openness to God. Those who would make idols of the self, wealth, power, or those who respond to God with *non serviam,* "I will not bow down," cannot achieve true and lasting happiness.

Mary's beauty lies in her total openness to the All Beautiful God. Her beauty reflects a marvelous simplicity and clarity. She knows who she is and what she is, accepting herself as God's creature. She accepts that through God's goodness to her, all generations will call her blessed (cf. Lk 1:48). Insofar as creatures can, Mary accepts and controls her own destiny, freely choosing its course as willed by God.

Mary consented to God's coming into the world, becoming man through her. As believers, God invites us to make Christ come alive today by our witness of faith. As a woman of decision and great faith, Mary helps us in the difficult faith-decisions of our lives.

Beautiful in her freedom and strength, Mary was also a quiet, humble and sensitive woman. Her uniqueness derives not from power but from goodness, love and the fullness of *charis*—grace. Her uniqueness does not remove her from us; it draws us to her. It delights us as it delights God.

He has shown might with his arm;
He has confused the proud in their inmost
thoughts.
He has deposed the mighty from their
thrones
and raised the lowly to high places.
The hungry he has given every good thing,
while the rich he has sent empty away.

(Lk 1:51–53)

PRAYER

God of mercy and love, we give you thanks for
the power you have shown in our lives: the power
to change our hearts, the power to be merciful and
loving in our lives, the power to lift the poor out of
poverty and bring them alive to you.

And so we praise you, Lord, for you have given
us every good thing and all that we need to believe
in you. Fill us with your Holy Spirit, as you filled
Mary. Help us to believe as she did, and to have the
courage to make decisions that will allow you to
come alive in us and our world. Give us the peace
that comes from knowing we have done your holy
will. We make this our prayer in the name of Jesus,
the Lord. Amen.

*She made
an
independent,
courageous decision
and she stood by it
for a lifetime.*

THIRD REFLECTION

A WOMAN OF GREAT FAITH

After the Archangel Gabriel received Mary's fiat and left, the room remained exactly as it had been before and, by all appearances, Mary remained exactly as she had been. But human history would never be the same again. God had sent Gabriel to tell Mary that the Holy Spirit would overshadow her and she would conceive and bear a son. This son would be called Jesus and he would save all people from their sins. He would sit upon the royal throne of David, rule over the house of Jacob and his reign would last forever. He would be called Son of the Most High and Son of God. Mary responded as a woman of great faith, "Behold the handmaid of the Lord; let it be done to me according to your word" (Lk 1:38).

Mary believed, against all natural probability,

that within her womb lived new life, the beginning of the child who would fulfill God's promises and be called Son of God. How could she believe it? Because she was already a woman of great faith, she believed that God is faithful. Mary believed that the messiah, the Redeemer and glorious king promised to her ancestors, would one day come. She believed in the limitless power and wisdom of God. He could do all things. God could even make her the instrument of his saving power.

In the stable as she laid her newborn son upon the straw of a manger, Mary believed she was placing there God's Son, Christ the new Adam, Jesus the saving power of God. When she and Joseph went to the temple to offer the sacrifice of two turtle doves for purification, Mary believed she was presenting God with his own Son. As she raised Jesus, she believed she was teaching the new Solomon to talk, the new Adam to live and God himself to pray.

The ordinariness of Christ in his humanity probably challenged Mary for her whole life. Was he really Son of God and Savior of the people? Would the expected messiah call others to meekness, humility and forgiveness? Would he establish his kingdom on love, as Jesus taught?

Mary's faith remained firm although tried from the time of stillness after Gabriel's departure, to that moment on Calvary. As Christ hung on the cross, she stood by her son believing, despite the darkness of that Good Friday afternoon. Mary, the mother of Jesus and first disciple, believed and loved her son totally. Imitating Mary means believing through all of life's joys and sorrows.

Living in a world that has a narrow, self-centered vision, concerned only with the pleasures and problems of the here and now, makes it difficult to think of our future life. This kind of vision does not reach out to God, to the hope of eternity, to a universal family. As Christians our vision needs to be focused on God, on the truth that God created us for friendship with him in time and in eternity and that we are accountable to him.

Despite our daily struggles we continue to believe that God lovingly cares for us more than for the birds of the air or the flowers of the field. God counts the very hairs on our heads because he cherishes us. God is always with us, always cares for us, always reaches out to us with an all embracing love.

We need to believe in ourselves as God believes in us! God has created every human person in his image and likeness. When God sees us he sees his image and likeness, his beloved children, the sisters and brothers of Jesus; he sees the unique and special individuals he created. If God created everyone in his image, then we also need to believe in others. Looking on everyone as God does, we can believe in their goodness as his creation and in their capacity to build up God's kingdom of love. We believe that a love as indomitable as one that dies on a cross, conquers all.

Our dream for life is an eschatological dream—a dream of joy and perfection that lies beyond this life, an unimaginable joy and perfection which we describe as "being with God" or "reaching our heavenly home." But we also believe that the human situation of this world is perfectible, and so we strive to make it a better, "more human" place to live. We dream and work for a world where every person's basic human needs will be met, where society respects the human dignity of every person, where the social order is based upon the truth that every person is the image of God.

Our faith reminds us time and again that our minds and hearts cannot be fixed only on the things below. Our vision of faith, fixed on those "eternal things" above, seeks to move us beyond

The Virgin Mary,
who at the message of the angel
received the Word of God
in her heart and body
and gave Life to the world,
is acknowledged and honored
as being truly the Mother of God,
our Redeemer.

"passing things" to loving kindness, generosity, unselfishness and creative ambitions.

Faith is intangible, often obscure. It challenges us to look beyond what we can touch and see and hold. For this reason, faith always involves a leap into the dark. But it also opens the door to light and to achievement. Mary did not limit her belief to what she could see and touch. Even when she could not understand events or see the way ahead, she believed in God's wisdom, power and goodness. She trusted God and willingly risked everything when she said yes.

In the darkness of inaccessible mystery she could say: "Yes, Lord, your way is my way. I will take your Word into my life and into my womb. I believe that through me, your lowly servant, your eternal Word will echo throughout the world and throughout all of history." And through her response of faith Christ came into the world, the beginning and the end of all things, the divine model for our human existence, the Truth we believe, the Way we follow, the Life we are to live.

Imitating Mary's faith in our own lives can unleash a powerful, creative force. It can give direction, energy and purpose to our lives, impacting society. What we believe determines the direction and quality of our life; what the people of a nation believe determines the direction and quality of society. Mary's example challenges each of us to be persons of faith.

> He has upheld Israel his servant,
> ever mindful of his mercy;
> even as he promised our fathers,
> Abraham and his descendants forever.
>
> (Lk 1:54–55)

PRAYER

God of mercy, hear our prayer, for we are your people: the people who have heard and believed your promise. We want to trust you with our faith, with our lives. Give us your Spirit, that we may believe as Mary did. Help us to say, "My soul gives praise to the Lord, and my spirit rejoices in God, my savior" (Lk 1:46–47).

Uphold us, Lord, as you upheld Israel, your servant. When our faith is weak, remember the promise you made long ago. For we believe in you with all that we are, and we pray for a deeper faith, in Jesus' name. Amen.

My Child,
at twelve you are a man the law says.

Only twelve,
my heart says yes, with tears.

Now, man-child, you are lost
your father and I searching.

How empty the crowded road,
how lonely the caravan without you,
breath of my breath.

Wherever you are there is my heart.

While I search, I surrender.
You are not mine, so very much mine,
you are the Father's.

"Where are you?" my heart cries.
But also, wherever you are
I love you.

In a stable you tugged at my breast,
so small, so warm. God's beautiful Gift.

How closely I have held you.
Yet with Simeon's sword
set you free to walk as you must.

Child of mystery, man of mystery
I accepted you in love.
But only then began
to learn the meaning of love.
Sorrowing, your father and I will search.

But I know, my love,
that you must walk all the pathways
of all the world, and of all time.

FOURTH REFLECTION

MARY'S ASSUMPTION—
SIGN OF HOPE FOR THE WORLD

Shortly after the annunciation Mary proclaimed her "Magnificat." Her words echoed a theme of thanksgiving for release from captivity found in Psalm 126. She said: "My soul gives praise to the Lord, and my spirit rejoices in God my savior.... For the mighty One has done great things for me..." (Lk 1:46, 49). Mary identifies herself with those who revere God: the hungry, those who seek God's mercy, those who trust in God's promises, those who wait. She rejoices as one who understands that the Lord has done something through her for all humanity.

Psalm 126 also prompts us to think of Mary's assumption into heaven. We might well imagine Mary, the poor woman of Nazareth, arriving at the glory of heaven after the pilgrim journey of her often difficult life. She may have said, "This is like a dream. My mouth is filled with laughter and my tongue with rejoicing. I say to the nations: the Lord has done great things for me! The Lord has done great things for me, indeed!"

As Mary was assumed into heaven, entering body and soul into glory, she became the sign of what the Church and every just person will be at the end of time.

Mary's bodily assumption signifies hope in a world that often exploits the human person. Prostitution and pornography sell bodies as commercial commodities with no reverence or respect for the dignity of human persons. In Third World countries, human bodies, especially those of children, waste away from malnutrition and starvation. In military States, bodies are mutilated through torture or worn out in work camps. In war torn areas, bodies are shot or maimed. As long as nuclear weapons exist, they threaten to instantly incinerate countless millions.

Mary, taken into heaven body and soul, is a sign to the world that every human being—body and soul—deserves profound reverence and respect. The assumption reminds us that one day—like a dream—God will bring all exiles home and fill their mouths with joyful laughter. In this life we may often go forth weeping, carrying the seeds of our sorrow, but the assumption of Mary into heaven assures us that a day of harvest and rejoicing will dawn.

Mary assumed into heaven is the same woman who proclaimed the "Magnificat." The daughter of an oppressed and captive people, one of the *anawim*—the poor remnant—Mary felt full solidarity with the oppressed, the lowly, the hungry and the poor. She rejoiced that the coming of the messiah would set her people free. Mary's prayer of trust in God's fidelity was also a prayer for her people: "He is here! The promise is fulfilled! He will depose the mighty from their thrones; he will raise up the lowly."

Entering heaven, Mary's joy embraced all people. In the "Magnificat" she said, "He is here!" and in her assumption she said, "You too will be here— I am merely the first. You who sow seeds in tears will harvest in joy with me."

Mary assumed into heaven stands as a sign for all those who live in obscurity, anguish and pain, those whose lives seem meaningless. She shows us that God makes dreams of peace and happiness a

*Mary's glory
and exaltation
in the assumption are
a sign of hope for us.*

reality. Mary's glory and exaltation in the assumption give us hope. Although exalted before all others, she is a woman, a human person, one of us.

PSALM 126

When the Lord brought back the captives of
Zion
we were like those dreaming.
Then our mouth was filled with laughter,
and our tongue with rejoicing.
Then they said among the nations
"The Lord has done great things for them"
The Lord has done great things for us.
We are glad indeed.
Restore our fortunes, O Lord,
like the torrents in the southern desert.
Those who sow in tears shall reap rejoicing.
Although they go forth weeping,
carrying the seed to be sown,
they shall come back rejoicing,
carrying their sheaves.

PRAYER

Lord, we give you thanks this day, for you have done great things for us. When we were lost in our limitations, you found us and set us free. When we found it difficult to believe, even in ourselves, you filled us with laughter and showed us how to love.

Help us now, Lord. Teach us to pray as people of faith. Give us your Spirit that we may believe as Mary did. We make our prayer in the name of Jesus. Amen.

FIFTH REFLECTION

MARY'S LOVE FOR ALL PEOPLE

From the Gospels of Matthew and Luke we learn that Mary freely chose to become Mother of God, that the Lord was with her, that she found favor with God, and that she was a virgin. To whatever extent we may speculate concerning each account's style of presentation, the inspired Word assures us that these facts are true.

When we go beyond scripture, everything concerning Mary's life moves into the realm of conjecture. This is my conjecture: Mary felt great pride in her Jewishness, of being a member of a certain people, and she possessed a deep love for her people. She knew their history as God's chosen people. Mary also knew well of God's promise to her ancestors: a messiah would come from the house of David.

With all her heart, Mary wanted the messiah to come. She desired the promised messiah so intently that she found favor with God. Certainly no creature could merit the honor and grace of becoming the mother of God, but perhaps God chose her above all women because of her great love for her people and her longing for the messiah. Mary's desire for the messiah *was* God's favor to her and the *way* he was "with her."

The archangel conveyed God's invitation of motherhood to Mary in messianic terms: "Behold you will conceive in your womb and will bear a son, and you shall name him Jesus. He will be great and will be called Son of the Most High, and the Lord will give him the throne of his father, David. He will reign over the house of Jacob forever and his kingdom will have no end" (Lk 1:31–33). As a Jewish woman, Mary understood that the archangel was speaking about the messiah, the descendant of David and ruler in the house of Jacob. When Mary said *yes,* she was not saying merely "let this child come to me," but "let this child, the messiah, come to all the children of David; let him come to the House of Jacob, called Israel. Let the messiah come into the world."

In the "Magnificat," Mary cried out with joy for

all her people: "My soul proclaims the greatness of the Lord.... Holy is his name.... He has come to the help of Israel his servant, mindful of his mercy, according to the promise he made to our ancestors, of his mercy to Abraham and to his descendants forever." No one was ever closer to the people of Israel than Mary of Nazareth.

At the Incarnation Mary probably focused her concern on her people, Israel. But perhaps she also understood that the coming of the messiah into the world would bless all humanity.

As she followed the universal teachings of her son more closely, she realized that Jesus, the Savior, had come for the salvation of all people. "This is the will of my Father, that everyone who sees the Son and believes in him should have eternal life" (Jn 6:40); "When I am lifted up from the earth, I will draw everyone to myself" (Jn 12:32); "They will come from east and west and from north and south and recline at the table in the kingdom of God" (Lk 13:29).

Through the eyes of Christ, Mary began to see a new Israel, a people who reached from the beginning of time to its end, who came from all places and cultures. She understood that everyone was a brother or sister of Jesus Christ and that his people were her people. The longing she felt for the salvation of Israel grew into a longing for the salvation of all humanity. When she stood at the foot of the cross and Jesus said, "Behold your son," Mary accepted all humanity as her own children.

By God's favor and her Son's command Mary extends her maternal care to everyone. She cares for you and me. This woman of Nazareth comes close to all people through her Son, in accord with God's plan.

> Now, Master, you can dismiss your servant
>   in peace;
> you have fulfilled your word.
> For my eyes have witnessed your saving deed
> displayed for all the peoples to see:
> a revealing light to the Gentiles
> the glory of your people Israel

PRAYER

Gentle God, hear our prayer. We are the people who have heard your word and believed. We have witnessed your saving deed and can testify that you alone are God, worthy of all trust. You are salvation for all peoples. Save us, Lord, from all that ties us to sin and keeps us from full belief. Give us your Spirit, as you did to Mary, and help us to believe, understand and live as she did. We make this prayer in Jesus' name. Amen.

MAGNIFICAT

My soul gives praise to the Lord,
    and my spirit rejoices in God my Savior;
Because he had regard for the lowliness of his
        handmaid,
    behold, henceforth all generations shall call me
        blessed,

For the Mighty One has done great things for me,
    and holy is his name,
And his mercy is from generation to generation
    toward those who fear him.

He has shown might with his arm,
    scattered the arrogant in the conceit of their
        heart,
He has pulled down the mighty from their thrones,
    and exalted the lowly,

The hungry he has filled with good things,
    and the rich he has sent away empty.

He has come to the aid of his servant, Israel,
    mindful of his mercy,
Just as he promised our fathers,
    Abraham and his descendants forever.

(Lk 1:46–55)

SIXTH REFLECTION

Our Lady of Sorrows

Michelangelo's *Pietà,* once marred by a vandal's hammer, is now restored and exhibited at St. Peter's Basilica in Rome. An invisible wall of plexiglass protects the statue, displayed in the nave of the church. Illuminated by a soft even light, the *Pietà* is tilted forward very slightly for perfect viewing. Lingering before the sculpture's poignant beauty, its meaning slowly and powerfully takes hold of the viewer's heart.

Somehow the genius of Michelangelo has made the marble supple and soft, expressing heartbreak. The large figure of Mary holds the smaller figure of the dead Christ in her arms. This perspective effectively depicts the enormity of Mary's grief over Jesus' terrible suffering in his passion and death.

Mary's right arm supports Christ's body while she extends her left hand as in an embrace, an offering, a gesture of immeasurable pain. She is every mother holding her dead child, every person who grieves for someone dear and departed, every man and woman grieving over lost dreams or shattered hopes. Mary feels the heartbreak of all humanity; she feels all the sadness of life.

The *Pietà* speaks the universal language of human anguish; it possesses a universal meaning as it silently utters the deepest human grief—a perfect mother grieving over her perfect Son, innocence sacrificed for evil, ultimate tragedy entirely undeserved.

In this painful scene, Mary appears once again as a woman of great courage and a sign of hope. Courageously Mary holds the lifeless body of her only child after he was taken down from the cross. Jesus endured the scandal of a criminal's execution and Mary, probably recognized by some as his mother, endured the ridicule, reproach and insults of the crowd. Perhaps she also received the pity of neighbors who knew that this widowed mother had only one son—and he seemed a failure. Mary bore in her arms the weight of her son, and in her tender heart the weight of her grief.

Mary stood on Calvary as a sign of hope in an apparently hopeless situation. What did Mary have left but a dead body? Where were Jesus' miraculous deeds, the awe-inspiring teachings, the words of love and forgiveness? Nothing ever seemed as hopeless as that moment, yet no hope ever burned brighter than Mary's. Even in the darkness of that Good Friday, Mary believed. With a human heart she grieved for her son. With a heroic heart she awaited the fulfillment of God's promise.

Simeon's prophecy concerning Mary was fulfilled: "You yourself will be pierced with a sword, so that the thought of many hearts will be laid bare" (Lk 2:35). Words from the Book of Lamentation describing Israel or Zion in her desolation may be applied to Mary: "Come all of you who pass by the way, see whether there is any suffering like my suffering" (Lam 1:12).

Mary's grief poured itself out as compassion, a grief endured for others. Her pain was centered on Christ and on us. She suffered because he was born in a stable, because he was misunderstood during his public ministry, because he was insulted and abused, because he died on the cross. And because Jesus entrusted each of us to her care, Mary grieves for each heartache of ours.

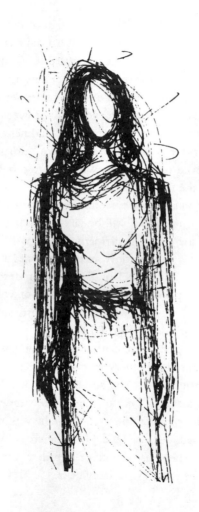

When she stood
at the foot of the cross
and Jesus said,
"Behold your son,"
Mary accepted
all humanity
as her own
children.

Mary was like a tree whose roots drive deep into the earth and always move toward water, the source of life. She was like a flower turning for life to the sun and rain. She lived deeply rooted in prayer and in openness to God—waiting, listening, ready. By all appearances this humble and hidden woman of Nazareth lived an ordinary life. Perhaps Mary never expected that God would choose her, but her life of waiting, listening and readiness prepared the way for her "yes." She continually moved toward God, the source of her life.

Mary's readiness allowed God to speak his word to her and to gift her with the Word Incarnate. Her readiness to do the will of the Father gave her strength to walk the road to Calvary beside her Son. Mary became the new Eve beneath the cross as she held in her arms the slain body of Christ, the new Adam. Under the cross Mary wept for herself, the lonely woman of Nazareth; she wept for the newborn she once held in her arms, nursed at her breast, taught as a boy, accompanied as a man. She wept for her dead son. Bearing in her arms the weight of our redemption, Mary wept for all humanity.

Prayer

This child is destined to be the downfall and the rise of many in Israel—a sign that will be opposed. And you yourself will be pierced with a sword so that the thoughts of many hearts may be laid bare (cf. Lk 1:34–35).

Loving God, your word to us had laid bare our thoughts and feelings concerning ourselves and our faith. Send forth upon us your Spirit of truth. Help us open ourselves to you in complete faith and trust, as did Mary. We make this prayer in Jesus' name. Amen.

EPILOGUE

A Pastoral Reflection

As a boy beginning grammar school, I was a member of Visitation Parish in Chicago. The parish and the neighborhood were almost synonymous, since Irish Catholics predominated in the area. Visitation Parish was like a world in itself, which one was born into, moved into from one of the several nearby parishes, or came into from Ireland itself. When someone died, they were waked and buried from Kenny's tiny, crowded funeral parlor. From Kenny's to Visitation Church—it was the only way to heaven!

The massive Gothic-style church, a grand building made of gray weathered stone, had a wide granite stairway that led up to the main church. The building seemed to loom over the traffic moving on the boulevard below—a "boulevard" that was really just two streets divided by a green parkway with one street carrying traffic eastward, the other westward.

On Sunday mornings most people walked to church in family groups. The whole neighborhood bustled with people coming and going. With Masses celebrated in the upper and lower church and with people moving up and down the grand stairway, in and out of the building, the church resembled a beehive buzzing with activity.

The Irish-born pastor also acted as "lord and master" of the neighborhood, the political wards, the local police and fire stations. Politicians and officials paid him deference. People came to him looking for work, promotions, settlements of domestic disputes, money, spiritual advice, help in *any* trouble…. He had all kinds of power in God's world and in ours—power which he used with prudence and true compassion. People loved him in a reverential way.

When the month of May arrived, the pastor organized the crowning of the Blessed Virgin on the parkway in front of Visitation Church. With the May altar set up on the green grass, the 1,500 children from the grammar and high schools—girls in white dresses and boys in white shirts—looked like a garden of gardenias around the statue of Mary. Many of the people in the neighborhood—parents, relatives and friends of the children—lined the sidewalks. Even amid the noise of the nearby parkway, the recitation of the rosary reverberated over the din of the traffic. As hymns like "Mother Dearest, Mother Fairest" soared to the sky, one young girl, chosen as queen of the May, placed a crown of flowers on the statue of the Blessed Virgin. Visitation Parish was honoring its mother; we were celebrating our faith.

For some time now Visitation Church has been changed into an inner-city parish. Many of the Irish Catholics moved away; they themselves changed. The neighborhood is perhaps only six to eight percent Catholic. The high school is closed. The parish and grammar school struggle for existence. The old neighborhoods have vanished— those small worlds with their sanctions, supports and limitations. One wonders if children are still being taught about Mary, the rosary, the communion of saints and the love of the heart of Jesus? Today it seems that many are strangers to Mary and the rosary, to the marvelous reality of the living community that is in heaven, on earth and in pur-

With the May altar set up...
a crown of flowers
was placed
on the statue of the Blessed Virgin.

gatory, and strangers to the devotion and powerful symbolism in the Sacred Heart of Jesus.

In every time and age our Catholic devotional observances—associated with certain months of the year—serve as important teaching tools. In October, the month of the rosary, children and adults learn about the rosary, taught how to pray it, and perhaps pray a part of it at home, in school or at their parish church. With its falling leaves, melancholy November is the month of the "poor souls." We are reminded about the communion of saints—the link between the living and the dead, the living and the saints in heaven, the living and those who suffer in purgatory. The month of May links springtime flowers, songs, festivals and, most importantly, our humanity with Mary. In June, with its growing crops and the stirring of new life, we remember the tenderness and warmth of God's life-giving, healing love symbolized in the Sacred Heart of Jesus.

Devotion is a wonderfully human element of religion and life that develops in the midst of a prayerful people. The Church offers us a rich "language for prayer: words, melodies, gestures, iconography" (*Catechism of the Catholic Church,* 2663). From this eloquent language, born of tradition and faith, comes our devotion to Mary. She is that wonderfully human person whom God chose as mother. From the annunciation to Calvary, Mary lived as a mother and disciple. At the cross she became mother to all of us, the brothers and sisters of her Son. As the mother who leads us to Jesus, she is the faithful disciple, full of grace, whose life and example show us the way to her Divine Son.

Pauline
BOOKS & MEDIA

The Daughters of St. Paul operate book and media centers at the following addresses. Visit, call or write the one nearest you today, or find us on the World Wide Web, www.pauline.org

CALIFORNIA
3908 Sepulveda Blvd., Culver City, CA
   90230; 310-397-8676
5945 Balboa Ave., San Diego, CA
   92111; 619-565-9181
46 Geary Street, San Francisco, CA
   94108; 415-781-5180

FLORIDA
145 S.W. 107th Ave., Miami, FL
   33174; 305-559-6715

HAWAII
1143 Bishop Street, Honolulu, HI
   96813; 808-521-2731
Neighbor Islands call: 800-259-8463

ILLINOIS
172 North Michigan Ave., Chicago, IL
   60601; 312-346-4228

LOUISIANA
4403 Veterans Memorial Blvd.,
   Metairie, LA 70006; 504-887-7631

MASSACHUSETTS
Rte. 1, 885 Providence Hwy.,
   Dedham, MA 02026; 781-326-5385

MISSOURI
9804 Watson Rd., St. Louis, MO
   63126; 314-965-3512

NEW JERSEY
561 U.S. Route 1, Wick Plaza,
   Edison, NJ 08817; 732-572-1200

NEW YORK
150 East 52nd Street, New York, NY
   10022; 212-754-1110
78 Fort Place, Staten Island, NY
   10301; 718-447-5071

OHIO
2105 Ontario Street (at Prospect
   Ave.), Cleveland, OH 44115;
   216-621-9427

PENNSYLVANIA
9171-A Roosevelt Blvd., Philadelphia,
   PA 19114; 215-676-9494

SOUTH CAROLINA
243 King Street, Charleston, SC
   29401; 843-577-0175

TENNESSEE
4811 Poplar Ave., Memphis, TN
   38117 901-761-2987

TEXAS
114 Main Plaza, San Antonio, TX
   78205; 210-224-8101

VIRGINIA
1025 King Street, Alexandria, VA
   22314; 703-549-3806

CANADA
3022 Dufferin Street, Toronto, Ontario,
   Canada M6B 3T5; 416-781-9131
1155 Yonge Street, Toronto, Ontario,
   Canada M4T 1W2; 416-934-3440

¡También somos su fuente para libros, videos y música en español!